Divine Inspirations

SAUNDRA D. McLESTER

WESTBOW
PRESS
A DIVISION OF THOMAS NELSON

Divine Inspirations
Copyright © 2012 Saundra D. McLester

WestBow Press books may be ordered through booksellers or by contacting:

WestBow Press
A Division of Thomas Nelson
1663 Liberty Drive
Bloomington, IN 47403
www.westbowpress.com
1-(866) 928-1240

ISBN: 978-1-4497-4876-0 (sc)
ISBN: 978-1-4497-4875-3 (e)

Library of Congress Control Number: 2012907172

Printed in the United States of America

WestBow Press rev. date: 5/24/2012

Be Still

As the years passed, I bellowed out "Be still, be quiet, and listen". These commands were given to my three daughters and two sons. Consequently, I learned to listen to the rustling sound of the leaves, the whistling of the wind blowing through the trees, the song of the birds, and the voice of serenity as the water ran over the rocks. Life is a poetic scene, a gift to grasp love, happiness, peace, and joy. It is given to the young, middle-aged, and old alike…to all! I can always hear the words of 1 Kings 19:12 echoing in my ear which were spoken from the mouth of my father, who was a preacher. I continued to listen as that still, small voice said to me," Be still and know that I am God"- Psalms 46:10. I reverted in response from that moment of awareness, "Speak Lord, for thy servant heareth"!

Contents

Introduction

I grew up in Winston, Georgia, a small country town thirty miles west of Atlanta. I lived with my father, mother, and nine siblings. I am a preacher's kid (PK). My dad, the late Elder Joseph McLester, was a preacher by God's calling, and a farmer by trade. My mother, Christine, was a faithful wife, mother, and prayer warrior!

REST IN PEACE

My dad took his entire family to Sunday school and church every Sunday. He preached the Word, and instilled in all of us to "Hear the Word, obey it, and apply it to our life daily."

The prayers, teachings, and guidance from my God-fearing parents impacted my life, making me the woman I am today. Their teachings of love for God, self, and others endowed me with freedom and self-expression. I soon became my authentic self.

I recall another valuable lesson dad taught ... priorities. God should always be first, family second, and people third. Dad taught me to love everybody! He demanded that this principle be kept in perspective.

I know that my dad loved God first because he always displayed it in his preaching, teaching, writing, and love for all mankind; especially his family. I believe it rubbed off on me!

My passion to inspire, motivate, encourage, and love everybody is depicted in my writings.

Furthermore, my heart's desire is to impart the love of God from my heart to my audience's heart. My prayer is that, by faith, my audience will understand that mere reading of the words is not enough, but that the practical application of the words read is of utmost importance to me. I hope that the words will "come alive" to be food for your soul! For more than twenty-five years (since 1985), God has bestowed upon me His creative power to write these "Divine Inspirations." My life is a living testament as I continue to fulfill my hopes and dreams. By faith, I shall live a "Purpose-Driven Life," a life that will glorify and honor God!

Action in Christ

Feel the spirit; see the movement of God. Let it come alive in your soul. Be still, and know that He is the Great I Am. Let the Master exhilarate your total being—make it more than just a notion.

Do not alienate your brothers or sisters (in Christ or blood kin). Remind them that they are alive and well and that they are moving by His Spirit. Tell the good news to everyone you meet; enforce and reinforce to all that you may greet!

Live with all the positive reinforcements within your heart. Reverence the Creator of life—mover of mountains, the power source, the one and only superhero, and the one with all the action—the biggest verb in all the force!

Angels

I may not see the angels with my natural eye,
But I believe they are watching me from the sky!

We need them for protection all through the day;
They are good for all of us, always and in every way!

I thank God for my family and for all His love.
I thank Him for all of His blessings sent from above!

The angels are there when I work, sleep, and travel too;
They are the best guardians of all time for me and for you!

AS You Are

Wounded, broken, desolate, and desperate, God is waiting with outstretched arms, petitioning you to come as you are! You may be heavy laden with cares of this life, with troubles leaning on every side. Do not be deceived by Satan's lies and trickery, telling you that Jesus does not care. Jesus loves you as you are. Forget about yourself, and swallow your pride!

Excuses about the proper attire to wear to go to God's house to worship Him should not be made. He is beckoning, "As you are!" Man looks at the outer appearance, yet God looks at the heart. We concern ourselves with what people say, while He is patiently waiting for us. Believe in Him, and trust Him as you are. Jesus is so long-suffering, His salvation He'll impart!

We sometimes wonder why life seems so unfair, blaming someone else for our downfalls. You cannot save yourself; only God can save you—as you are! The road less traveled is the one we should be on. Veer not to the left or the right, but go straight ahead. Do not look back; move on up the King's highway. Know that the roadmaster is saying, "Go with me as you are; I will never leave or forsake you, day or night!"

The moment of truth is sure to come, for God hates sins in our lives. He is always there, ready to forgive; receive His mercy as you are! To pray, fast, and obey the Lord is a must after we give our lives to the Savior. There's no other way to live. Happiness, peace, and joy are in the Holy Spirit. We made up our minds to come as we were, and now we're reaping the benefits of His righteousness and divine favor!

AT&T

(Adhere to Triumph or Tragedy)

Which one will it be? When tragedies come, will you adhere to the bad news negatively, or will you be so overjoyed with faith in good news that you will let the triumphs make you disregard all the negative blues?

The outcome depends on how we react to what we hear or see! We may hear something sad or bad; we may weep or drop our heads in empathy. We can also react positively—even in the midst of the tragedy.

Surely we always want to have victorious living, yet sometimes in life, there will be ups and downs.

We were not promised a life of flower beds of ease—and yes, we were promised provisions for a way of escape, regardless of success or hard times. Know and believe that if we repent of our sins and endure, we will wear a crown!

Checklist for Your Spiritual Journey

Hat (helmet)—for salvation (Ephesians 6:17)

Clothes (garments)—for praise (Isaiah 61:3)

Robe (breastplate)—for righteousness (Ephesians 6:14)

Sword (of the Spirit)—for speaking the word(s) (Ephesians 6:17)

Belt/girdle (loins)—for truth (Ephesians 6:14)

Coat (shield) or outer garment (toga)—for faith (Ephesians 6:16)

Shoes (feet shod)—for preparation of the gospel of peace (Ephesians 6:15)

Jewelry (spiritual ornaments) (1 Peter 3:3–4)

Come, Go with Me

Freedom affords us the opportunity to go where we want to go. Some choices may be good and some not so good. We come, we go, that's just the way it is …

But as for me, I was glad when they said unto me, "Come, let us go to the house of the Lord." That is the best place that I know to go—God's house. The church is His.

There is a still better place called heaven. This earthly sojourning is just temporary. We are just practicing here, dressing up for that eternal life.

My prayers are for every woman, man, and child to go—go to a far, far better place than down here. The doors swing open on welcome hinges, ending all strife.

We do not have to contend with sadness, pain, or sorrow. Once we get there, all earthly trials will be gone. We will not have to cry or die anymore.

The sun (Son) will always shine; the streets shine too. The gold will be everywhere; the rivers will be crystal clear. You can shop to your heart's content in heaven's grocery store!

Come, go with me, for Jesus said, "There are many mansions there." I hope to see my loved ones marching around God's throne. There will be no more marriages there—no wife or spouse.

Only the family of God and His children will be up there. Now is the time to prepare for such a glorious place. Give your life to Him, and let us go together to my Father's house!

Distance

Space is distance; distance is not measured in space
Nor in how far or how long!
Hearts keep us close together—mighty and strong.

We may be miles and miles apart in the natural sense—
Lonely for each other's touch.
The spirit is what counts; the flesh should not matter as
  much!

Yes, we miss seeing the sight of one another—
The quality time we spend with family and friends.
The sweet words said and heard are music to the ear,
Yet somehow the closeness remains, whether far or near.

Reach out in love and understanding; keep the message clear.
The message is: love cannot be measured in time or space.
You may be there; I may be here, whatever the case.

The distance is not the case, but caring is.
Assuredly, we can feel our heartbeats of daily living
  struggles—
I cry, you cry; I hurt, you hurt and feel what I feel.
What matters most is that in time, we will heal!

So, onward Christian soldiers, we have to start out
  somewhere.
We all have a charge to keep. Come, let us travel the spiritual
  road.
Do God's will, and we'll all get there!

Don't Risk (Wrist) Living without Him

God is all thumbs up!
He is Alpha and Omega—the index, too!
He is the Trinity (three in one)—Father, Son, and Holy
  Ghost!
He reigns (rings) supreme!
His love has no color line (even pink).
Do not risk (wrist) living without Him!

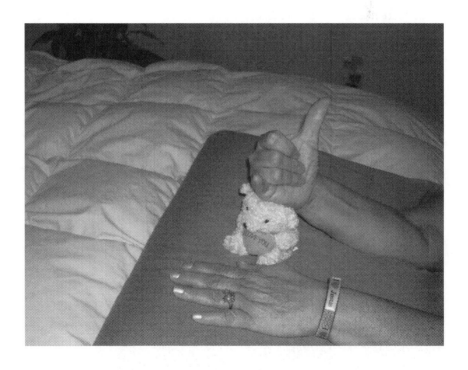

Endure

Psalm 27 commands us to "wait on the Lord and be of good courage"; be obedient, be patient—Endure.

The "Race of Life" is not won by the fast one or the strongest survivor, only the ones who endure.

To endure is to rise above all the circumstances; to let your faith excel; to trample the doubt, fear, and unbelief under your feet … Good things come to those who wait; your needs God will meet.

Patience is a virtue, long-suffering is a "fruit"; a spiritual fruit that Christians need; the "charge" is here to possess them all; Love, Joy, Peace, and Happiness too. We all need to endure, indeed!

Sometimes up, sometimes down, the problem is, we do not enjoy the wait. We murmur and complain and question God with "Why, why, why?" instead of praying to our Lord and acknowledging "Oh Holy Thy!"

Whatever we want, we want it now. We long to make it happen, sometimes too quickly. We want Jesus Christ to be like a microwave; pop it in a few minutes and it's out. That makes Him sick!

Jesus tells us to "not be anxious for anything" yet we ignore His command. He also said, "Let your requests be made known," according to His will and not your demand!

God patiently waits for us to get it together and give our hearts to Him. Of course, we become weary in a short time ... acting as if we have obeyed and are doing just fine!

None of these negative actions are good signs of endurance; to last we must have godly characteristics, living and thinking just like Jesus did for sure. Letting go and letting God work in us through the Holy Ghost is all we need to Endure!

Flaky Friends ...

Think only of themselves (selfish)
Do not act in your best interest
Do not show themselves friendly
Pretentious; not really "for real"
Apt to judge; but not out of love
Show very little empathy/sympathy
Not very genuine

Forgiveness

With a heart to show all the love within me, I live …
And that same heart, to admit I have wronged you, says, "I forgive."

Once, twice, three times is not enough to prove how sorry I may be.
Many, many times are needed for forgiveness to be felt effectively!

Thanks for the chance to forgive, and be forgiven too …
My conscience is clear in me, and also toward you!

GOD *in Route 66*

In Genesis: He is the beginning; The Great 'I Am'. In Exodus: He is the leader of the exit; from bondage into the Promised Land. In Leviticus: He is the lawgiver. In Numbers: He is the census taker for His people. In Deuteronomy: He is the author of the Ten Commandments. In Joshua: He is the Victor and the Victory; and the walls of Jericho came tumbling down. In Judges: He is the 'sitter-on-the-throne' judging righteously.

In Ruth: He is the head of the family; filling the mother(s) and daughters-in-law with His love. In First and Second Samuel: He continues to manifest His power and glory to Eli more than once. In First and Second Kings: He is the King of kings and Lord of lords. In First and Second Chronicles: He is always in divine order. He speaks to His people, commanding them to "humble themselves and pray". In Ezra: He is over all the Scribes. In Nehemiah: He is in control of the 'Watergate'. In Esther: He is always prevailing for those who honor, obey, and trust Him (i.e. Mordecai, and the Queen). In Job: He is the only one that is able to put the hedge around those He loves, and the only one that can give life and take it away.

In Psalms: God sings to us morning, noon, and night. In Proverbs: He speaks to us poetically. In Ecclesiastes: He is always our "preacher". In Song of Solomon: He is the lover of our souls. In Isaiah: He is our prophet in a major way. In Jeremiah: He had to cry because of our sinful, rebellious ways.

In Lamentations: He loves us so much that He sent Jesus, who laid down His life for our sins. In Ezekiel: He is the wheel-in-the-middle-of-the-wheel. In Daniel: He is the fourth person in the fiery furnace; the lion tamer too. In Hosea: He is the lover of all nations and families, (husbands, wives, and children). In Joel: He is pouring out His spirit upon all flesh. In Amos: He is the 'battle axe in the time of a battle'. In Obadiah: He tells His prophets to prophesy to His people. In Jonah: He made the creatures of the sea. In Micah: He communes with the one who thinks he is so important, and with the peons too. In Nahum: God is always 'on the scene' (a stronghold), sitting high, looking low. In Habakkuk: He is the greatest visionary. In Zephaniah: He comes through for His humble servants. In Haggai: He may not come when we expect Him to, but He is there nevertheless. In Zechariah: He is 'Hosanna' in the highest. In Malachi: He is the giver and controller of our finances.

God continues His pathway through the lineage of Jesse, David, Joseph, and His virgin mother Mary. In Matthew: He manifested himself in the flesh, the child of the Holy Ghost. In Mark: He was transfigured before a few of His disciples. In Luke: He is the greatest physician. In John: He is our salvation worldwide. In Acts: He is an awesome apostle. In Romans: He was and is the lawgiver, the grace giver and the savior of all people, of every nation.

In First and Second Corinthians: God is the one true teacher and instructor of life, love, and marriage; and He backs up His leadership and authorship with proof of His power to all His students, that will learn of Him. In Galatians: He is our vineyard maker. He gives us our 'good fruits'. In Ephesians: He is the Church: Body of Christ. In Philippians: He is the strong tower, the pillar of the church. In Colossians: He is the 'breach' between man and our Creator (the One who can work it out for us). In First and Second Thessalonians: God is Paul's instructor, letter writer to the church of Thessalonica; letting Paul and us know explicitly that He will 'shorten the time for the elect's sake', so that His people can make it to heaven. In First and Second Timothy: He is the writer/sender of more letters to the church, telling His saints how to see, live, study, and conduct themselves as the 'body of Christ'. He also writes to us about His second coming. In Titus: He is the 'commander in charge', commanding His saints to "contend for the faith that was once delivered to the saints" (of old). In Philemon: He is the only one who stands in the gap for us. In Hebrews: He is our faith builder. In James: He is our healer, our 'pure religion', our tongue tamer, and our WORD. In First and Second Peter: He is our ending search for life both naturally and spiritually, our eternal life; our freedom is in Him. He is our life, liberty, and pursuit of happiness; we find peace through Him.

In First, Second, and Third John: GOD IS LOVE; we love Him because He first loved us. In Jude: God is the winner at the finish line. In Revelation: He is the Divine Revelator, the Alpha and Omega, the Beginning and the End, the First and the Last.

Note: I praise and thank God for giving me this "Revelation" of Him. He has assisted me with memorizing all 66 names of the books in the Bible. God reveals His character in all 66 books. He is our 'character-builder' everyday! He also revealed to me that He is a 'two-fold' God. For example, we learn and are taught by Him at the same time. He is awesome in every sense of the WORD!

Moreover, through the Holy Spirit's leading, I recorded His (The Great I AM) teachings from Genesis to Revelation without having to open my Bible a single time! Hallelujah! God will enhance our memory and write His 'words upon the table of our heart'. However, we must allow Him to. After my divine encounter, I gained more knowledge about God's character. He revealed His Glory in the 'physical' route 66. I was in Texas when He poured out Himself in me to 'write what the Spirit said'; after which I traveled to New Mexico, not realizing that these two states (out of four) were actually route 66! Praise be to God!

HAPPINESS Is ...

Having an
Accentuated
Positive
Personality
Individually
Needing to be
Entwined with your
Soul
Salvation

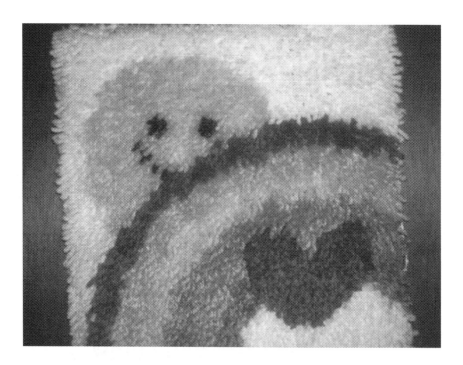

History Repeated

Wars, rumors of wars
Earthquakes in divers places
Nation against nation
Fear written on all our faces …

Disease, Sickness, Pain, and Hurt
Famine, Pestilence, Turmoil too,
Problems mounting, pressures rising—
Sometimes we don't know what to do …

Parents against children,
And most of them are gone astray,
Heaven and Earth are going to pass,
But God's word is here to stay!

All these things that are happening,
Read your Bible; they've happened before.
God warns us that in the last days
Perilous times will come, I mean galore!

Think about the crisis in the Middle East,
Men thinking they have power, pride getting in the way.
God's word has to be fulfilled;
It doesn't matter what man may say.

Our military loved ones, who fight for world peace,
Countless brave young men, numbers untold,
Prepare to defend themselves and other countries too.
People, let me tell you, "God is in control"!

How Long?

Impatience is a negative attribute. We want what we want, when we want it; we do not want to wait: we ask consciously/subconsciously, how long?

Notice all the "W"s, and note that it is eight (God's number of completion): Now believe that the longer the wait, the more we will end up strong!

On the other hand, "patience" is a true virtue to those of us who wait. We take on eagle's wings. We run and don't get weary. We walk and don't faint.

We do not worry about how long it takes. We bask in our ability to "stand still"; yet remind ourselves there is not a word called "can't"!

Sometimes the odds appear to be so against us. We wonder, ponder, and let time be a factor. We say within ourselves that "time is of the essence."

We factor "when and where and how" into our "living webs"; never to consider that time is not in our hands. Instead, we complain, and do not bother to usher in God's presence!

The longer we wait, the better our fate. Be of good courage and of good cheer. The Master's timing is never our timing. Hold on, wait until the end.

We may immediately get a "yes" or a "no," or maybe a "wait." The question is not "How long?" but it should be "Will you, Dear Lord, give me the patience I need to wait for what you send?"

In This Life

In this life, some rain will fall, troubles stand tall,
Tests and trials will come. We ask, where do they all come from?
In this life, there is sunshine too, for me and you.
The rainbow appears after the storm; then comes the calm.
In this life, we experience many things that life may bring,
Sometimes up, sometimes down; always smile—never frown.
In this life, there are seasons, a time, and a reason;
Darkness prevails at night, but the next day brings light!
In this life, there may be negatives all around, yet positiveness always abounds.
The good far outweighs the bad; happiness outweighs the sad!
In this life, we do things we regret. We complain and we fret.
Just be thankful and grateful too; do not let "the enemy" tell you what to do.
In this life, there is always hope. Jesus will help you cope.
Don't worry, don't despair, the "troubleshooter" is always there!
In this life, we need faith the size of a mustard seed, yes indeed.
The mountains will move out of your way—just believe and pray!
In this life, stop to smell the roses, stand erect with the poses.
from our beginnings to our endings we will see, life is so beautiful, we all must agree!

Just for Today

We cannot put off today for tomorrow because tomorrow is not promised anyway. Just live for today.

Live today as if it were your last day on earth. Make it fulfilling and thrilling, just for today.

Do not worry about tomorrow, or what it will bring; the moments become sensational when you live just for today!

Count all the blessings of the day. Yesterday was then, tomorrow is the future, today is nigh; do not sigh, but live for today.

Surely rain will come and storms too … Clouds break through every day to send what they will. Be glad, just for today.

Seasons change; winter brings cold, summer brings heat. April showers bring May flowers. Let the "Dayspring" come for today.

Time is of the essence; use it wisely. Lend a helping hand, tell someone you love them. Be kind, just for today!

Stop to smell the flowers, to hear the whispers in the wind. Behold the beauty of nature; appreciate the splendor just for today!

The things we see are temporal; the things not seen are eternal. Release the fear of what tomorrow holds; believe for today!

Today is a gift to all; a promise fulfilled. Live it without doubt, with a shout; rejoice in the present, just for today!

Life According to the Soaps

These are the *Days of Our Lives*;
We only have *One Life to Live*.
Teenagers now are *The Young and the Restless* and
are not getting prepared to go to *Another World*.
I pray that *All My Children*
will be led by the *Guiding Light*.
As the World Turns, mankind is so sick and diseased that they
head straight for the *General Hospital*.

The Doctors are baffled and confused and they *Search for Tomorrow*, but today has not ended. Please let's pray and love one another, because the *Edge of Night* approaches.

Meet Me in the Middle

My friend, whether you attest you are the first, last; beginning or ending; measure-up to one-fourth or three-fourths, just meet me in the middle.

Through the thick and thin; through the 'School of Hard Knocks": what I need my friend, is for you to meet me in the middle.

Does not matter the few or the many or how long your friendship has been; let us continue to love each other and somehow meet in the middle.

Let us cherish the good times we shared; reminisce the experiences of our past; and do not give or take from the other, but always meet in the middle.

As disagreements come, and we realize they will, let us remind ourselves that "right is right" and "wrong is wrong," and just meet in the middle.

According to the book of Proverbs, "A friend loves at all times." Jesus is a friend that sticks closer than a brother; let's just meet Him in the middle.

And we have always heard that a "friend in need is a friend indeed." A friend can be our mother, father, sister, or brother; just meet in the middle.

Life's journeys can seem complex, my friend. We may search high and low for answers to all life's problems. But we must remember to allow Jesus to meet us in the middle.

Let Him come amid our relationships; thank Him for allowing us "to be." Ask Him to let us always meet in the middle.

Relationships of all kinds will always work out all right, as long as we humble our hearts, keep positive thoughts, and say to each other, meet me in the middle!

Modern Times

People are so modern that they have forgotten where they come from. They don't realize that God has brought them from a mighty, mighty long way. He has brought them from …

Lamps to Light

T-Model to Cadillac

Woodstove to Gas or Electric

Bicycle to Motorcycle

Scrub Boards to Automatic Washer

Press Iron to Electric Iron

The Farm to the Store

Home Remedies to Modern Medicine

Shack to Brick

Manual to Remote Control

People used to love, and now they hate.

They used to be happy, but now they're sad.

They were in the light but have traveled to the darkness.

They would visit their neighbors; now they don't. Everything has changed, but God remains the same!

Nature's Beauty

There is in abundance beautiful scenery to behold in just one
  day;
Sunshine, blue skies, flowers, trees, and God's awesome
  wonder shown in every way!

It does not matter where you live, where you work or play.
Just look up and see all the wonderful sights that are on
  display!

The list of beautiful things on this earth will take a lifetime to
  see: mountains, valleys, oceans, seas, trees, oh, the splendor
  of His love for you and me!

Sounds of waterfalls here and there warm the heart and
  soul.
Birds chirping day by day, bestowing peace and tranquility—
  what a joy, what a delight to hear and see so much beauty
  unfold!

The clouds so brilliant, so white, so perfect;
Be awestruck by the "heavenly" view, appreciate the sunshine,
  the rain, the snow, whatever the Creator sends, be happy
  with life; enjoy the scenery, whether many or few!

Then there are the moon and the stars that glow so radiantly
  in the night;
They light up the sky with a breathtaking message; telling us
  how blessed we are to be illuminated with their shining so
  bright!

Everything around us is beauty; some of it may be manmade. Bask in its beauty; let the radiance be a part of your daily routine, a routine of gratitude to the true source: "Power Aide"!

If your travels take you somewhere in your city or state, it does not matter where. Whether you go far north, south, east, or west, around the world and back again, take the time to behold Nature's Beauty, don't hesitate!

Oasis

Calmly, peacefully, the desert waters flow …
A haven of solitude is in the atmosphere,
Smiles on people's faces, eyes all aglow!

There is a peace that surpasses all understanding.
Come, let us reach out to grab life and a
Positive attitude, a release to all that is demanding!

For how do we redundantly say "I need my space" …
Constantly creating our day-to-day comfort zone, overlooking
The weightier matters that confront the human race!

The Creator and maker provides tranquility within.
We will surely reap these bountiful blessings as we help a friend!

As we always trust our faith and the higher power …
Surround ourselves with love and concern, humbly submitting
our time: more than just an hour!

The welcome call we long to hear …
"Well done, thou good and faithful servant" will be an "Oasis" (calm) within itself,
and it is hopefully very near!

To strive to be good stewards should be our goal …
and to lend a helping hand, we must always do.
Complacency must cease, and our arms must unfold!

Provisions for working the "harvest" have been made …
The harvest is plenteous, but the laborers are few.
The seed and the sower will produce a good grade!

For all who are wondering, "What do I do?" …
Stop for a moment to reflect; God, the Oasis, the Power, the Glory, has made the way for you!

Oh What a Friend

I. The song says, "What a friend we have in Jesus." Additionally, the Word declares, "There is a friend that sticks closer than any brother" ...

Having such a friend as this, brothers and sisters, let us love one another.

II. We have heard over and over again, "A friend in need is a friend indeed." Though the barrels may get low, the bills stacked high ...

Depend on the One, the only One who will never leave nor forsake you. Always count on that best friend; your needs He will supply!

III. I remember my mother saying back in the day, "Girl, you cannot rely on your so-called friends, they will disappoint you and let you down" ...

When I grew up and became an adult, I understood just what Mama meant. Upon calling on "those friends," they were gone, nowhere to be found!

IV. And the friends I did find had excuses; questions too. They wanted to know, "When will you repay this loan?"

Those "friends" did not have patience, not to mention trust; obviously, they did not read what the money said: "In God we trust," because of the groans and moans!

V. The lender and the borrower must believe. Believe on Jesus who will always be there for whatever the need; we can always count on Him for help ...

He owns the cattle, the houses, and the land. Everything belongs to God. It does not matter how many times we need or how much we need; our wonderful friend waits for us to ask; He will honor our requests, step by step.

VI. Friends come and friends go. Good friends may last a while. Surely times do tell; real friends give their shoulders to cry on ...

You talk, they listen; this makes the heart glad, yet there is one that is better than all the rest, I say again, and again, my friendship with Him has fully grown!

One Step Closer

Life is a journey: birth; crawl; make one step …
Two steps, three, and four. The goal is to reach the finish
line.
Keep persevering; do not look back; get one step closer with
God's help.

The race is not for the swift or the strong …
But for those who endure. The starting line may have been
for three laps; now down to two, one; keep on running.
The end is not long.

Stay focused on the 'prize.' Yesterday is gone …
Tomorrow is not a promise, yet we hope to see it. Each passing
day we get closer to our destiny—ten, nine, eight, one to
go—to reach home.

Draw nigh to the King. He will draw nigh to you …
Step by step we will make life's journey. We may have begun
many years ago, or weeks, or days; it does not matter how
long or how few.

Keep on keeping on. With hope we will win …
Love is the energy that gives us strength. The motivating to
not stop or quit helps because where there is life, there is
hope—to the end.

No need to veer to the right or to the left …

But go forward; move in the right direction. You are further now than when you first began. Be confident. Believe in yourself.

Do not worry: we all have come so far by faith; one more day …
One more step; make preparations to go to a better place;
From earth to heaven we are closer to the "end." Let us pray.

Our Destiny Is but a While Away

Who knows where our destiny lies?
Only God.
We wait and we wonder when and sometimes why.
For we don't know our fate; only the Lord, only Thy.
The Lord is on his throne judging right.
He knows all, sees all, and hears all.
So just watch and pray, and please don't forget to love!
Then, when our destiny comes,
we will have already done what we were supposed to have done.

Praise of Preparation

I. Throughout history in our worship experience we have heard the "Song of Preparation." That's wonderful, but why not a praise, a shout-out to God as we prepare to hear the engrafted Word, the only thing that is able to save us? When the praises go up, the blessings come down. So we have heard that phrase throughout our "saved" lives and this is true … The blessings are in the praise, lifting up our hearts to God in adoration and absolute trust!

II. Clap your hands, stomp your feet, make some noise, say Hallelujah. Let God know that you are ready to hear and obey. Always be mindful too that God wants us to remember that obedience is even better than sacrifice. As we enter into worship and bring the "Sacrifice of Praise" into His house, let us honor and love Him. Forget about yourself and pray for the deaf ears to be unstopped, the sins and weights laid down; keeping our eyes on the prize!

III. Lo, Jesus is with us always, even until the end. Make ready the food, where we'll never hunger, the water where we'll never thirst. "Bread from heaven, feed us till we want no more." Bind the cords of selfishness, loose the chains of fear …

IV. Continue in prayer, praise, and prepare to receive. Receive in healing, salvation, victory, and all that God has to give. Stay there; keep wearing the Garment of Praise. Listen for the Word to shower down from heaven; it is nigh thee, in your heart. Just hear!

Psalm 116 (Paraphrased)

KJV

"My Breakthrough"
Wed. (12/17) p.m., Th. (12/18) a.m.

I.   "I love the Lord because he has heard my voice and my supplications." The Lord heard my "voice" from my heart! I could not speak because my natural voice box was not working, due to laryngitis (inflammation of the larynx). I cried out to Him with thanksgiving and praise for manifesting His unconditional love to me.

II.   "Because He hath inclined His ear unto me, therefore will I call upon Him as long as I live." I was on my bed of languishing, and God heard my despairing cry!

III.   "The sorrow of death compassed me and the pains of hell gat (found me) hold upon me: I found trouble and sorrow." Satan tried to come with evil/negative thoughts: I would cough myself to death; I had a dreadful disease (AIDS, pneumonia, etc.). I was wrestling with fear, doubt, and unbelief.

IV.   "Then I called upon the name of the Lord: Oh Lord, I beseech thee, deliver my soul." I had to pray, pray, pray for deliverance. "You shall not die, but live," saith the Lord of Hosts!

V.   "Gracious is the Lord, and righteous; yea our God is merciful." The Lord had mercy on me! He reassured me that though sickness and pain may come in the night season, that I could call Him anytime, day or night, sick or well, for an answer!

VI. "The Lord preserveth the simple; I was brought low and He helped me." The Master humbled my heart, healed my trembling body, and made me ready for a peaceable rest in Him!

VII. Return unto thy rest, O my soul; For the Lord hath dealt bountifully with thee." My soul was eased, my body relaxed. Rest to my mind and body finally came about 4:00 a.m. that Thursday. The Lord poured out His healing grace upon me. I closed my eyes, overwhelmed with so much joy and peace!

VIII. "For thou delivered my soul from death, mine eyes from tears, and my feet from falling." My God did a threefold miracle in less than three seconds! Naturally, I did not die, I did not cry, and with the small amount of strength I had in my left knee (from knee surgery a few days before), God gave me more strength to praise His holy name! Spiritually, my spirit man was revived and "out of my belly flowed rivers of living water!" (John 7:38). He made "my feet like hinds' feet" (Psalm 18:33). Glory, Hallelujah!!

IX. "I will walk before the Lord in the land of the living." I must walk in the spirit! I must tell the Good News to God's people, at His command.

X. "I believed, therefore have I spoken; I was greatly afflicted." The Lord reminded me a few hours later that I had spoken to Him with my "heart" in my affliction, and because of my belief in His word, He came to my rescue!

XI. "I said in my haste, all men are liars." God continued to minister to me, reminding me "not to put my trust in man, whose breath is in his nostrils," but to trust Him for ALL my needs!

XII. "What shall I render unto the Lord for all His benefits?" The answer to this question is PRAISE! The blessings are in our Praise!!

XIII. "I will take the cup of salvation and call upon the name of the Lord." Jesus told His Father in Luke 22:42, "Father, if thou be willing, remove this cup from me, nevertheless not my will, but thine, be done." Our prayers should always be, "Not my will but thine be done."

XIV. "I will pay my vows unto the Lord now in the presence of all His people." The Lord continued to speak to my heart to tell His people that "paying vows" was more than just monetary; but that we as His chosen disciples must "pay" with the sacrifices of our praise, our hearts must "pay tribute" to our risen King! Also, at this point, He let me know that I had been "honoring Him with my lips, but my heart was far from Him." His command for all of us is to stop the "lip service" and give our hearts wholly and completely to Him!

XV. "Precious in the sight of the Lord is the death of His saints." The Lord let me know early that Thursday morning that if I had departed this earthly life the night before, my physical death would have been precious to

Him! He said, "I gave you a new life, hidden in me a long time ago." Tell my people that "Real life begins when their journey here on this earth ends!"

XVI. "Oh Lord, truly I am thy servant, I am thy servant, and the son of thy handmaid; thy has loosed my bonds." We must tell Jesus that we will do His bidding. When we follow His commands, we are set free from bondage! The sins of omission, fear, and complacency are forgiven!

XVII. "I will offer to thee the sacrifices of thanksgiving, and I will call upon the name of the Lord." I called upon the name of the Lord with my whole heart! God got my attention by taking away my natural voice, in order for me to know that "sacrifices of thanksgiving" come from the heart!

XVIII. Note: This verse is the same as verse 14. Read Psalm 22:25 and Jonah 2:9.

XIX. "In the courts of the Lord's house, in the midst of thee, O Jerusalem, Praise ye the Lord!"

The Lord's house is in my heart and soul! After praising the Lord with all my "heart" and soul, He led me to read and "hear" Psalm 116 in order for me to "see" why He allowed me to experience what I had seen the night before. Jesus told me to tell what He allowed to happen to me, to His people as a testimony of His goodness, mercy, and glory!

"PRAISE YE THE LORD!"

Reach Out/Up and Touch

The sky is the limit …
So do not worry, don't fret.
God has never failed you yet.

Somewhere down the line you will see …
Your mission work was not in vain.
Many lives you will touch; for Christ is great gain.

Think about your spiritual journey …
Reach up; touch the hem of (Jesus') garment,
Reach out in faith and love, show them both, live it!

The "unknown" sometimes makes us fear …
God is universal, sitting high, looking low.
He is here, in the airplane, even in Moscow, don't you
know?

"My granddaughter, Tiera, you are an honoree …
I thank God for you. Only what you do for Him will last.
Your destiny is "light," your future bright; do not live in the
past.

Always keep the love and prayers of family close at heart …
Remember the solid foundation teachings you have
received.
Let God work through you, to bless the children, for in Him
you have believed.

And sweetheart, never forget to take the Lord everywhere you go …

Never look down on anyone unless you are picking them up.

Stay positive, stay focused on Jesus: He drank from the bitter cup!"

Real-Ease and Release

I. Experience a "real-ease" (release) when you let go of doubt, fear, and unbelief … Holding on to the 'negatives' only causes grief.

II. Stop moaning, complaining; get rid of the lack of faith, hope and charity … Do not pretend; be "for real"; speak with clarity.

III. The race is not won until all come to the finish line; release the adrenaline, let it flow … Release false beliefs; do not allow them to grow.

IV. Never be "at ease" with whining, come on now; regarding anything in life at hand … Live in "the now"; join the choir or a band.

V. Yes, get on the "bandwagon," and ride the "Mighty High" … Restrain your lips from speaking guile; let wisdom come in your life, to inspire.

VI. Always keep a "new lease" on life: take it as it comes … There will be ups and downs. Just make them all experiences to learn from.

RE-A-SON

Whether rhyme or "reason," we are here on earth for but a
   season.
-AND-
Our purpose "for being" is regarding His Son …
-A-
Son that was given: out of a great love for mankind; an only
   begotten child, a
-SAVIOR-
Who died on the cross for our salvation; and
-WAS-
Born of a virgin mother (Mary); a Son
-GIVEN-
of the Holy Spirit, and no other. Jesus nailed our sins to the cross
-FOR-
Mankind to live again
-OUR-
Peace is upon Him; our
-SINS-
Are pardoned through Him,
-JESUS CHRIST-
Our Superstar;
-OUR-
Answer and Awesome Ruler; our
-KING-
He gave His life a ransom. He
-IS-
all we need. Believe that
-HE-
is our all and all. He gave us faith the size of a grain of
   mustard seed.

"Relationships Are Like a Remote Control"

1. We think we can turn them on and off when we get ready.

2. We think we can "Zoom" in and out of one another's life without any concern for one's heart.

3. We think we can "Pause" and not complete the relationship we started so sincerely.

4. We think we must "Rewind" when all we need to do is just "Fast-forward"!

5. We think we can just "Stop" and go on to another relationship.

6. We think we can just "play" with each other's feelings (heart, soul, and mind) and expect a big laugh in return!

7. We think we can "Record" all the things we want to watch later and "Eject" the source when we are finished!

8. We think we need the "Remote" to always be there by our side in order to "use it" as often as we deem necessary!

Repose

Go ahead; let the body "die out" to sin; awake, come alive to
spirit, a soul that wins.
Arise; get up, be sober, be vigilant; don't wait: and do not let
the adversary (the Devil) determine your fate.

The body is the temple for the Holy Spirit to dwell; the
"spiritual house" needs to be garnished and cleansed, to
sell.

The Word commands, "to present our bodies as a living
sacrifice" …
Let go, let God live in your heart and soul, is true advice.

Furthermore, the "Master" who can indwell, makes an
appeal …
"Will you come out of 'repose' (resting) to be filled?

"Filled with the true Light, the real life of love and peace;
Have a mustard seed of faith in Me; and sin will cease."

The harvest is plentiful, the workers are few; no time for
sitting and complacency: let Him arise in you.

Stand tall; believe that salvation is free to all; repent (believing
that Jesus died for our sins), and you will not fall.

For He died and rose again on the third day: He ascended
into heaven, then sent the Holy Spirit to stay.

We are all zombies (spiritually dead), until we ask God to forgive ...

Forgiveness is granted, we are "born again" ... that's when we live!

See God's Glory

Through pain, turmoil, and confusion, See God's Glory!

Life contains heartbreaks, trouble, and tears, but See God's
Glory!

Do not question, why me? Why did this happen? Just see
God's Glory!

Even in the midst of life's perplexities, don't fret: See God's
Glory!

Some way, somehow, through faith and belief in an

Eternal God, the sorrows and hurts will not be as trying as
we

Empty our hearts in praise and worship, knowing that Jesus

Gave His life for us. He died for us to have life! Let us

Obey His will (His Word is His will), and commit to being

Disciples; follow His footsteps, trust Him for

Salvation, and lean on Him when we are weak …

Giving Him all the praise in the ups and downs,

Loving Him just for being God and not like man.

Oh taste and see that He is good; His mercy endureth
forever!

Righteous in all His ways … and

Yes, when your eyes are opened to His truth and your faith is
not blind, you will See His Glory!

SOUL MATE

Serious
Opportunity to …
Understand your …
Lover with …
Mature
Attention and …
Teaching
Each (other)

Spiritual Detox

Take a minimum of thirty minutes to all day/night (always needed—and no "as needed") of prayer, praise, and Bible reading and study as your "laxative." After cleansing, take a daily dose of "Inspirational Vitamins." The "Cleanser" is needed to "Wash-out" all negative infiltrations: Pride, Selfishness, Backbiting, Jealousy, Idolatry, Adultery, Fornication, Lying, Cheating, Laziness, and Complacency. The list will surmount only if you allow it to. Then, take a triple dose of God's Word to cleanse your mind: at least three times a day (always needed).

Read and pray in the spirit, Romans 8:6 to cleanse your mind, Matthew 7:3 to clean you out with his infiltration process through your belly, so the "rivers of living waters" can flow, John 7:38, and let the "spiritual laxative" cleanse your bowels (by faith all the filth has come through our bowels!). Colossians 3:12–13 commands, "Put on therefore, as the elect of God, holy and beloved, bowels of mercies, kindness, humbleness of mind, meekness, longsuffering, forbearance, and forgiveness"!

The cleanser is guaranteed to cleanse you from head to toe! It also works as a blood purifier (Jesus Christ)! Exlax ®, Correctol ®, Epsom Salt ®, or the "stuff in the green bottle" does not compare with this! This is the only sure cleanser: the real "Master" cleanser. Take it (by faith), and life will never be the same!

Spiritual Insight

I met a man the other day that was blind. After talking to him, I realized that he wasn't blind. He just couldn't see! You see, there's a difference: for many have eyes but are still blind because they don't have a spiritual mind. Some have ears but cannot hear. They don't know what it is to fear. It's all in the spirit and the soul—not the physical, because God's blessings are untold.

The Act of Forgiveness

My Friend,

I have demonstrated acts of kindness and acts of love, but I have had a "show-and-tell" attitude, demonstrating just how sorry I am for the way I have treated you so negatively.

I now ask you to forgive me four-hundred and ninety times (Matthew 18:21–22) for my mistreating you. I realize that love and kindness are good attributes, but they are not enough to complete the entire process of your healing. The 'act' of forgiveness (even when we need to forgive each other) makes us well again.

The Connection

The "Power" Source was there, is there, and will always be
    there …
Keep holding on to His unchanging hand, without a load of
    care.
'Tis between you and Jesus, nobody knows like you and
    Him …
You are "hooked up" always; your faith is not slim.
God is the same yesterday, today, and forever; His wonders to
    perform; blessings upon blessings, miracles too …
God performed them for me, and also for you.

I know you have told the story of Jesus and His love.
You are an inspiration to me; day and night …
You spread the "news" all right.

Your life is a testimony. You love the "Connector";
He loves you too …
Old things are passed away, and behold all things become
    new.
No matter the trial or tribulation, His love always seeps
    through …
And my friend, you know why? Because the "Connector" is
    in you!

The Forgotten People

Wisdom comes with age;
The elderly can probably tell us why the heathens rage.
Despite their knowledge and their wide grins,
Younger generations shun them, although it's a sin.

I have even heard them express their feelings:
"No one seems to care anymore
Just because they're old."
Take time and listen, hear them out as their stories unfold.

Because we can maneuver and move a little faster,
We grow more impatient with them not realizing their steps
  get slower and their eyes a little dim.

Do we stop to consider that these old "fogies" were young
  one day? As time passed, they became mothers, dads,
  grandmas, grandpas, and great grandpas. Sometimes, as
  much as five generations! Always keep in mind that if you
  keep on living you'll get there one day. Whether young or
  old, we did not come here to stay!

Young folks think they've got all the answers, thinking they
  are depriving an old lady or man of knowing anything
  about life …
Well, they knew before you got here, about life's sacrifice!

The I Z Es

Be mindful to realize that we must recognize where and who our supply comes from. We as humans are so quick to criticize one another. We are never satisfied with the small things in life; we always want to supersize what we already have been blessed to have. We tend to "cheat" on standardized tests; we think our hair has to be moisturized every day; our house has to be vaporized to clean out the germs; our words have to be emphasized to get our point across; we feel we need to have sympathized with our loved ones (especially our children) for them to act right. We "get going" in our motorized vehicles and head for our too publicized announcements of where we are going, especially for Wednesday night Bible study! Too often husbands and wives do not verbalize their true thoughts and feelings. We are scrutinized on our jobs by our employers when we are not performing to our fullest potential; we refuse to be baptized in the local church because of unbelief or thinking that getting baptized as a child is sufficient. We should be careful in regards to who we socialize with. We expect to be patronized after acting haughty or cold toward another; we are slow to let our fellow men know how much we care, by not communicating our empathized feelings. Once we have been revitalized and spiritized by the one and only Jesus Christ, then and only then will we become powerized to live just as we ought to live: just like Him!

The Real "V" Day

V – Victory is won

A – Answers to prayers

L – Love is …

E – Everlasting

N – Now (You and I know that) …

T – Tomorrow ("I will love you too, because") …

I – "I Am" said it. (He is God; He is good) so …

N – Never say "never" and

E – Every time you look around, see the beauty of His love; it is here, there, and everywhere!

The Way Down Is Up

A poem for depression

When you are feeling down, depressed, and in despair,
Look up, hold your head up, and recognize Jesus does care.

Realize this race is not given to the swift or the strong,
But given to the one that endureth, no matter how long.

"Trouble, trouble, so much trouble," we are quick to say.
"Trouble does not last always"; take life, day by day.

As you kneel there on your knees in humble submission,
Believe on the Heavenly King who grants remission.

He does not want you to worry, doubt, or fret
Or be cast down with "self-pity." He hasn't failed us yet.

Jesus Christ says, "Look up, for your redemption draweth
near. I sit high and look low; you have nothing to fear …

"I am the one who heals you, who knows all about you.
Just trust me; I have all you need, I will come through …

"I know all about your heavy burdens and load of care;
Always believe, I will not put on you more than you can
bear …

"I come to set the captives free and also the lost.
Keep my words in your head, counting the cost …

"I have already paid the price on Calvary long ago.
I am the Way, Truth, and Life; my Father said so …

"So, my child, while you are feeling 'down and out,' look to
the hills, I am your help and strength; only stay on your knees
and keep your faith filled!"

Time Changes

'Twas not the time gone by of great importance? For time is
of the essence.

From the cradle to the present, from the present to the end.

Good days and not so good days, make every moment count,
I recommend!

"Time is going to bring about a change,"

reminds me of a song someone made up years ago and I used
to sing.

The lyrics were profound and true.

Don't waste time worrying about changes in life; instead, take
each day as a gift anew!

Ponder not all the negatives; dwell on the positives. Live as if
time will be no more; walk in the pathways of life, and if
and when you stumble, get up!

The crooked will be made straight; open your heart to let
God sup!

The cells start the life cycle. They break up into millions of
pieces, forming the different parts of our bodies; for nine
months of time;

conception until birth, such a miracle divine! As time goes
on, we as His masterpiece begin to grow.

From infants to toddlers, from toddlers to preteens, growing
in body and mind.

Yes, changes occur over time, but life is never unkind!

Like the butterfly in its cocoon, locked up in its shell and in
the meantime,

it is waiting to break out, fluttering and floundering its
beautiful wings.

Time will not be waiting on us, so soar like the butterfly or
like the eagle; let your heart sing!

Man tries to make a change once a year by changing the clock
to "daylight saving time," but that really does not matter.
Like sand in the hourglass,

our lives are like vapor, and soon it will pass!

Do not let the changes in time change your mind. Whether
you hear the clock ticking or the bell tolls ringing, changes
will occur from time to time. Jesus commands us to "redeem
the time" (Ephesians 5:16). Accept all the good in life, and
you'll be just fine!

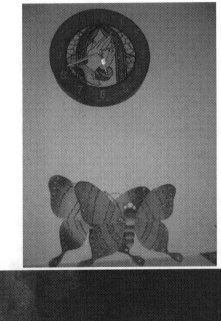

To Mother, with Love

Going back as far as Eve, Mother of all Living … Mother, you are just as worthy of praise; just as giving.

You gave birth to me, my brothers and sisters; all … how wonderful God's gift through this woman: Mom, you stand tall!

Mother, you've been there for us through thick and thin … with a smile on your lovely face and love within.

Without question, you are a rarity that cannot be replaced … a virtuous woman; your price is far above rubies; from beginning to end; the love I have in my heart for you can never be erased!

Dear Mother, you are a friend, teacher, and my confidante too … When I am feeling depressed, feeling sad and blue, I can always count on you to make my spirits new!

You are a praying woman who knows just how to get a prayer through … I realize you've had your share of life's ups and downs … Sometimes you worry, sometimes you frown!

But through all your trials and tribulations … and experiences of every kind, there is no comparison to the beauty of our relations.

My advice to all of us, your children, is to cherish, obey, and respect you, our mother, while life lasts, and always rely on God's grace … because when your mother is gone, only God can take her place!

What "Hand-some" Means to GOD

God will:
For our doubt,
He will "hand some" faith.
For our fears,
He will "hand some" courage.
For our unbelief,
He will "hand some" trust.
For our worries,
He will "hand some" prayer time.
For our impatience,
He will "hand some" longsuffering.
For our weakness,
He will "hand some" strength.
For our insufficiencies,
He will "hand some" grace.
For our loneliness
He will "hand some" more of Him!

Wind Song

The impetuous wind song, roaring in the day …
Whistling vehemently in the night, "Stop, Listen, and Pray."

I can hear the chorus's resounding voices of praise …
Praise to the Creator who sends His will, nights and days.

There is a message in the "Wind Song"; take time to hear …
Its impulsive strength may make you shiver, but believe its Maker is near.

Again, pay close attention to what the "sound" is saying …
"I am in control," says the Lord, "even as the wind is swaying."

There are many, many ways and days the Master lets us know …
That He made the world and all that is in it a long time ago!

Hear His beckoning call, "Come unto me, for I love you" …
Be still and know, His voice is in the whispers and the wind too!

The Wonderful Love of Jesus

The wonderful Love of Jesus is the sweetest Love for thee.
The wonderful Love of Jesus—no greater Love can be.
Each day think of Jesus and His profound Love,
How He died on the cross of Calvary and ascended to Heaven above.
Often our lives are filled with darkness and our hearts burdened with pain,
But just remember the wonderful Love of Jesus, Oh, praise His holy name!
Soon the day will break through and dark shadows will all flee away.
Then return the Wonderful Love of Jesus down on your knees to pray.

By Joseph McLester, Sr.

Mothers ...

A mother is a gift from heaven above
Sent to this earth to spread wisdom and love ...
God made her strong enough to withstand
All that she encounters, including her man ...
Her compassion is strong and her will even stronger,
Her patience is long and her love even longer ...
We should be thankful each and every day,
God blessed us by sending this angel our way ...
So today I want to say "Thanks, Mom" and "I love you very much."
I won't forget all those valuable lessons, and I'll always keep in touch!
May your day be filled with joy, and may all your wishes come true.
Keep smiling, sharing, caring, and remember, "I'll always love you!"

By Stuart McLester

In Just One Moment

Just before the sun gave grace to the earth's horizon on a cool, crisp Tuesday morning and while the air was still, the trees quiet and the birds forgot to sing.

A moment in time that seemed to last forever yet was only that—a brief yet dreadful moment. The earth came to a screeching halt, the angels commenced to sing, and the heaven peeled wide open.

My eyes began to fill, my heart began to break, and my tongue was paralyzed while my soul began to plead … "Wait!" with every ounce of my being I screamed from the inside …

"Not yet!" As streams of tears took over my cheeks, I looked up to heaven and wondered …

Does He even hear me when I say … "I need more time"?

How do I accept this moment gracefully and allow Him to employ His divine will?

How do I comprehend this temporary loan of my father, my hero, my teacher, and now, alas, I must accede to his return?

As dismal as this moment came, as joyous as it passed, the clouds began to roll and the smell of peace was in the air,

A faint smile upon his face as the world released his troubled soul.

The complex life that inhabited this being was now a story of the past like pages from a book.

Nevertheless, his memory is cherished in the minds and hearts of his five offsprings.

Although sadness and bitterness encompassed this moment, I cannot embrace the next.

His legacy of happiness, success, and a love for life supersedes all other moments. It will live forever within me.

As the air began to move again, the trees began to whistle and the birds remembered to sing,

The earth began to spin and the angels' voices became dim in the far distance,

I could see the heavens begin to close and at that moment my tongue gave way to words … "It's okay … now is your time to rest … I will see you later."

By Zenobia Thompson

Dedication

To the divine Inspirator, my Lord and Savior Jesus Christ, and all the heavenly host …
I could not have written the words of this book without the power of the Holy Ghost.

To my earthly father, Joseph, my mother, Christine, who were my prayer warriors, my friends,
I miss you two dearly.
God loaned me both of you up to fifty-five years of my life, until your end.

To my five beautiful children, Zenobia, Stuart, Duante', Leslie, and Patience: you are all an extension of that loan.
To my ten grandchildren, Tiera, Zakiyah, D'Aris, Courtney, Lexya, Deshon, Kyree, Brittany, Anai, and Duante' Jr.: I will always be there for you even after you are all grown.

Last but not least, to my three great-grandchildren, Amari, Aziyah, and Astyn:
My sweet little darlings,
Great grandma loves and adores you. Thanks for all your love too!

Acknowledgments

I am indebted to my heavenly Father for His good and perfect gifts. He is the "Author" and the Finisher of my faith, and I give Him credit as the Author of this book. I thank God for all His "Divine Inspirations" embedded into my heart and soul (spirit man), and making me the co-author.

Thanks to my audience for the opportunity to reveal God's love and awesome power operating in my life through my literary abilities.

I owe a debt of gratitude to my earthly father, Elder Joseph McLester, Sr., who, during his lifetime, dedicated himself to his children. Thanks, Dad, for your untiring love and motivation to live for Jesus, to preach His word, and to tell the world of His "Wonderful Love." Your wisdom and knowledge surely inspired me to be "just like you" as I follow in your footsteps as a God-inspired poet.

I thank you, my daughter, Zenobia, for all the encouragement and support you gave me during the writing of each poem. Thanks for the titles you gave me to write from. Your abilities to express yourself literally were handed down from God, your grandfather "Papa," and your mother (three generations of poets). I especially enjoy the words you wrote about your dad David in 2006!

Stuart, my second born, mere words are not enough to express my gratitude for all your hard work and dedication in pushing me to persevere and finish the work I started so many years ago. Thank you for coming up with the idea of you and I exchanging titles for our poems every week. Thanks for proofreading and typing every one of them! I will always cherish the words you wrote in that beautiful poem to me for Mother's Day.

Many thanks to my loving sister Regina for assisting me with your editorial skills and for all your prayers and encouragement. Thanks for being a blessing in my life.

Thanks Leila, for your editing expertise.

A special thanks to a beautiful young lady, Ashante, for all your help. I would not have been able to finish this work without all your ideas, creativity, and limitless knowledge of computers. Thanks also to your mother, Davina, my loving sister in Christ, my friend, for all your extra hard work.

I owe a debt of gratitude to all of my loving family, church family, and friends.

Finally, thanks my publisher, WestBow Press, who donated your time and talent in getting my book printed and into the hands of the public.

May God bless you all!